Eagles

Kate Riggs

seedlings

Published by Creative Paperbacks
P.O. Box 227, Mankato, Minnesota 56002
Creative Paperbacks is an imprint of
The Creative Company
www.thecreativecompany.us

Design and production by Ellen Huber
Art direction by Rita Marshall
Printed in the United States of America

Photographs by Dreamstime (Predrag1, Pressurepics),
iStockphoto (Ralf Hettler, igorkov, Eric Isselée,
Frank Leung), Shutterstock (Potapov Alexander,
bluehand, Critterbiz, FloridaStock, Eric Isselee,
Adrian T. Jones, Johan Swanepoel, Sergey Uryadnikov,
Jason Watson), Veer (cynoclub, visceral image)

Library of Congress Cataloging-in-Publication Data
Riggs, Kate.
Eagles / Kate Riggs.
p. cm. — (Seedlings)
Includes bibliographical references and index.
Summary: A kindergarten-level introduction to eagles,
covering their growth process, behaviors, the places they
call home, and such defining physical features as their
feathered bodies.
ISBN 978-1-60818-453-8 (hardcover)
ISBN 978-1-62832-041-1 (pbk)
1. Eagles—Juvenile literature. I. Title.

QL696.F32R54 2014
598.9'42—dc23   2013029066

CCSS: RI.K.1, 2, 3, 4, 5, 6, 7;
RI.1.1, 2, 3, 4, 5, 6, 7; RF.K.1, 3; RF.1.1

9 8 7 6 5 4 3 2

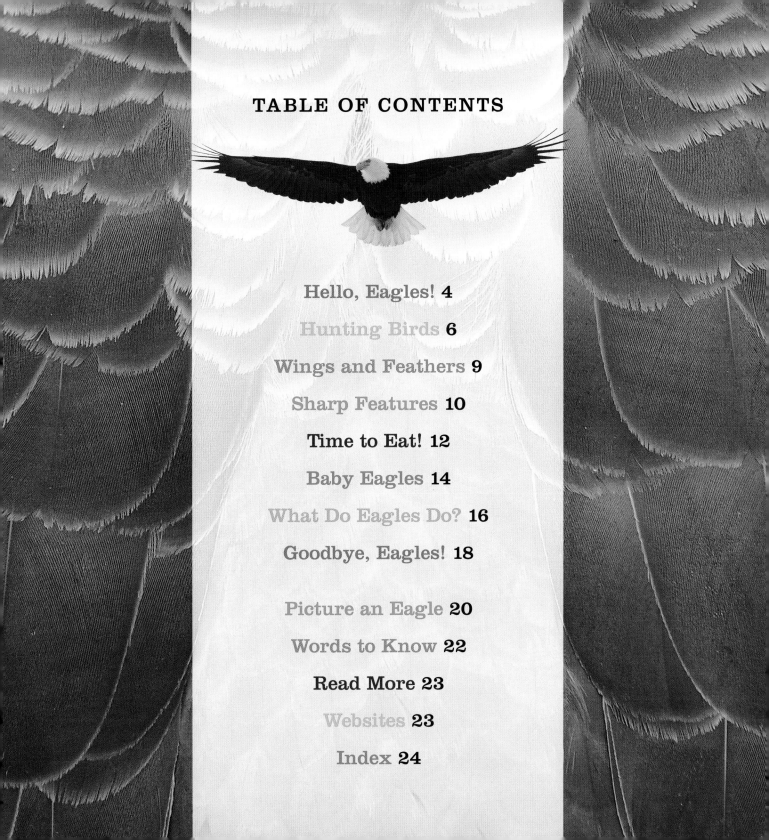

TABLE OF CONTENTS

Hello, eagles!

Eagles are large birds.

They live in
many places.
Many eagles
live near water.

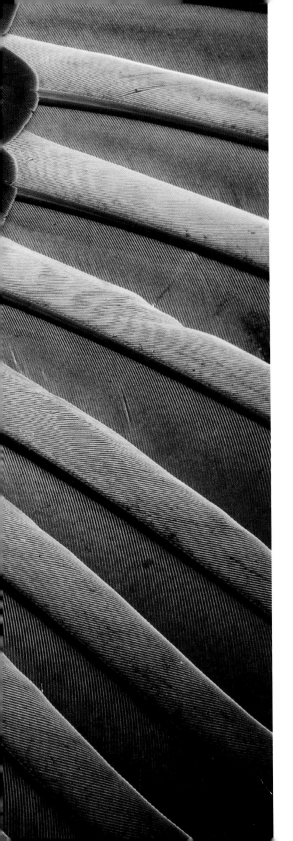

Eagles' bodies have feathers. The feathers are brown, black, gray, or white.

An eagle has claws on its feet. It has wings to help it fly.

Eagles eat
meat. They
hunt for mice
and snakes.

Some eagles
catch fish
for food.

Baby eagles are called eaglets.

They are born
in a nest.
Soon eaglets
get too big
for the nest.

An eagle flies in the air. It rests on a branch.

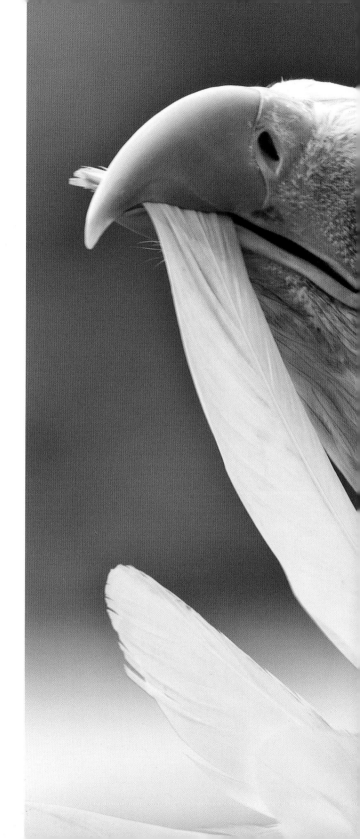

It cleans its feathers.

Goodbye, eagles!

Picture an Eagle

wing

eye

beak

feathers

nostril

beak

leg

claw

foot

tail

Words to Know

branch: a part of a tree that grows out of the trunk

claws: curved nails on the toes of some animals

feathers: parts of a bird's body that grow out of its skin

Read More

Macken, JoAnn Early. *Golden Eagles*.
Pleasantville, N.Y.: Weekly Reader, 2010.

Morrison, Gordon. *Bald Eagle*.
New York: Walter Lorraine Books, 1998.

Websites

Bald Eagle Handprint Craft
http://www.busybeekidscrafts.com/Bald-Eagle.html
Use your hand- and footprints to make a paper eagle!

Golden Eagle Videos
http://www.bbc.co.uk/nature/life/Golden_Eagle
Watch short videos to learn more about the golden eagle.

Index